Sudan

A Nation in the Balance

CRISPIN HUGHES/OXFAM

Contents

Oxfam UK and Ireland   **Chris Peters**

Sarah Errington/Oxfam

Faces of Sudan *(clockwise from top right):* Red Sea Hills; north Tokar; Bahr el Ghazal; Bahr el Ghazal; Red Sea Hills; Northern Darfur.

Sarah Errington/Oxfam

Sarah Errington/Oxfam

Sarah Errington/Oxfam

Crispin Hughes/Oxfam

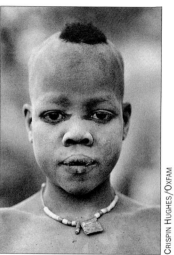

Crispin Hughes/Oxfam

2

Where rivers meet

Strolling along the wide corniche beside the Blue Nile in Khartoum, the capital city of the Republic of Sudan, is a pleasant way to take exercise. The pavement is shaded from the sun by leafy trees and there is a light breeze coming off the river. Above the trees and out over the river, kites ride the thermals, tracing lazy circles beneath a cloudless, deep-blue sky.

People throng the streets, pausing to greet friends or sit together on shady benches. The men are dressed in dazzling white hooded cloaks — *jellabiyas* — and turbans; the women are swathed in brightly coloured lengths of cloth. The atmosphere is easy and relaxed. To the visitor, Khartoum still conjures up a world that is quintessentially of the Nile: a world of deserts and tented encampments, and ancient civilisations and courtesies.

A little distance downstream from here, the Blue Nile will meet the White Nile. From Khartoum, the Nile, now one mighty river, will continue its journey towards Egypt, the Delta, and the Mediterranean Sea. Yet the Nile is not exclusively a river of the desert, or of desert peoples. The Blue Nile, rising amid the snows of the Ethiopian Highlands far to the south-east, and the White Nile, flowing out from Lake Victoria in Uganda to the south-west, pass through a great range of landscapes and cultures. The Nile flows the length of Sudan, through landscapes of dense jungle, vast swamps, grasslands, and desert on its journey northwards.

This diversity of geography and climate is reflected in the diversity of the peoples who live in these different regions. The Nile is a symbol of how such diversity might be reconciled, and how Sudan might one day be at peace with itself. For Sudan, apart from an interim period of peace (1972–1983), has been enmeshed in a chronic but catastrophic civil war between the government, based in the north, and anti-government forces, mainly in the

A Rasheida girl in Gabol Settlement, Red Sea Hills

SARAH ERRINGTON/OXFAM

south, since 1955, the year before Sudanese independence from Anglo-Egyptian rule. Currently, there seems little prospect of a lasting peace settlement.

The focus of this book is not, however, exclusively upon the war, but on the people whom it affects, and the lives of those who live on the fringes of a society that has been fractured not only by war, but by years of drought and harsh social and economic policies.

A forgotten country

Very few people visit Sudan, and those who do — apart from diplomats and a few business people — generally work for the UN or an international charity and are concerned with the logistics of humanitarian relief and development. So most of what is written about Sudan is buried in specialist journals or academic conference papers.

Beja girl in Rural Port Sudan

NIGEL CLARKE/OXFAM

Sudan made international headlines in 1984/85, when thousands of people starved in a drought and famine that devastated the Horn of Africa. But since then, Sudan and the Sudanese people seem fated to remain largely forgotten by the rest of the world, or perceived in terms of imperial history. For many British people, Sudan is still essentially a distant, desert country dimly recalled from their schooldays: General Gordon died at the siege of Khartoum in 1885 ... Sir Herbert Kitchener defeated the Dervish army at the battle of Omdurman in 1898 ... But why were they there? And what links, if any, do they have with modern Sudan?

This short book tries to fill some of the gaps. But it cannot hope to cover every aspect of the largest country in Africa. Instead it tries to give an overview of the country's history, geography, and political and social economy, seen from the perspective of ordinary Sudanese people. For if anyone is qualified to talk about Sudan, it is the people who live there: the tea seller in a Khartoum market, the school teacher in Bahr el Ghazal, the doctor in the bush clinic, the widow displaced by war, the chief of a tribe of nomads: the people who live or work on the social and economic margins of society, who are trying to find a voice for themselves and their communities, in a country that has been splintered by war for decades. What all of these people long for most is peace and stability, for without a lasting peace nothing else can be permanently achieved.

A land of diversity

Sudan is often presented in history books as two distinct entities: the north, prosperous and predominantly Muslim, and the south, neglected, exploited, and mainly Christian. Indeed, in the nineteenth century Sudan was, for a time, administered as two separate countries. Dividing the country into two halves is a convenient device still used by many writers on Sudan; it will occasionally be used in this book.

The reality is, of course, more complex than this neat separation implies, for Sudan is above all else a country of great variety and contrasts. If modern Sudan is to be understood properly, we must acknowledge its geographic, cultural, and historic diversity, and the variety of experience that this has generated. For this diversity has not only helped to mould the country and its peoples: it has also contributed to the problems that currently trouble it as a nation.

The largest country in Africa

The Republic of Sudan covers an area of about 2.5 million square kilometres (nearly one million square miles), approximately ten times the size of the United Kingdom. The geography and climate can be roughly divided into three broad bands: arid

Fellata Mbororo dancers at the festival of Eid, near Nyala, Southern Darfur

KAREN TWINING/OXFAM

5

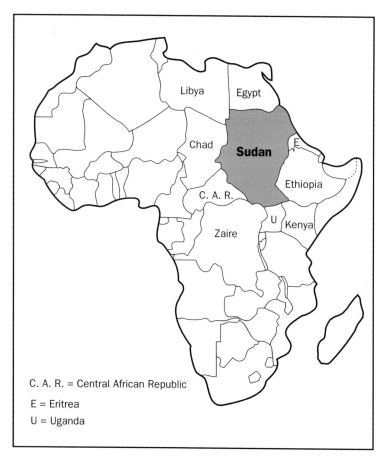

C. A. R. = Central African Republic

E = Eritrea

U = Uganda

deserts in the north; savannah grasslands in the central regions; and equatorial woodlands and swamp in the south, where annual rainfall can exceed 57 inches (1,465 mm).

Sudan borders the Red Sea to the east. To the north is Egypt; to the north-west, Chad and Libya; to the west, the Central African Republic; to the south, Zaire, Uganda, and Kenya; and, to the east, Eritrea and Ethiopia.

Sudan's current population of some 27 million people consists of 19 major ethnic groups that can be further divided into 597 smaller sub-groupings, speaking over 100 different languages. About 60 per cent of the population are Muslims; about 15 per cent are Christians; the remaining 25 per cent adhere to older religions. Most Sudanese, about two-thirds, are pastoralists or farmers, earning a bare subsistence in a harsh environment. Approximately two million people still follow a nomadic or semi-nomadic lifestyle, herding livestock.

Scratching a living from a harsh environment: ploughing at Sinkat, Red Sea Hills

SARAH ERRINGTON/OXFAM

A bird's eye view

The north and central regions

The central and northern regions of Sudan, particularly the lands along the river valley of the Nile, have been targets of invasion — and crossroads for trade and cultural contacts — for centuries. Egyptian, Greek, Roman, and Arabic cultures have all had a strong influence on these regions and their peoples. Through such contacts, successive urban civilisations have emerged throughout recorded history.

Apart from the fertile valley of the Nile, the northern region is remote and sparsely populated, with deserts stretching to the north and east for hundreds of miles into Libya and Egypt. Many groups live along the riverine valley, including the Nubians.

Economically, Sudan is dominated by the central region and the Three Cities that make up the capital city: Khartoum, Khartoum North, and Omdurman; most of the country's utilities, infrastructure, and communications systems are sited here. Khartoum is also the seat of government. In this region are based the middle-class professionals and business people who, it is estimated, make up one-tenth of Sudan's population. Between the Blue and White Niles, crops such as cotton and wheat are grown in the Gezira region, in the world's largest irrigated agricultural scheme under single management.

On the plains of the eastern region, between Khartoum and Ethiopia, Sudan produces most of its cereals on vast, mechanised farming estates. The crops are exported, mainly to Arab countries in the Middle East, and traded with parts of the country that are not self-sufficient in grain. On the Red Sea Coast lies Port Sudan, the country's one large commercial port, more than 1,000 km from the capital city.

The west

In this region live peoples such as the Nuba and Baggara in Kordofan, and the Fur and Messalit in Darfur. Farming small-holdings provides the livelihood for most people: growing millet, raising goats, and

Near Omeim village, north Tokar
SARAH ERRINGTON/OXFAM

A map of Sudan showing places and features mentioned in this book

collecting wild foods. About a quarter of the population are nomadic, herding camels and cattle. The western regions of Sudan range from unpopulated desert in the north, through poor sandy soils, to rich savannah lands on the borders with the southern regions.

The south

Beyond the vast swamps of the Sudd in the Nile Basin lie immense areas of savannah and forests. The population of the south largely consists of several distinctive Western Nilotic groups, such as the Dinka, Nuer, Anuak, and Shilluk. The Dinka are the largest single ethnic-minority group in Sudan. Cattle herding is the mainstay of their economy, together with semi-subsistence agriculture.

In a country where underdevelopment is the norm, the south remains perhaps the most underdeveloped area not only of Sudan but, arguably, of Africa as a whole. Years of neglect have meant an almost complete lack of investment and basic

JEREMY HARTLEY/OXFAM

Hilton Hotel, Khartoum

infrastructure — roads, schools, hospitals, local government, and industry. Since 1983, most of the meagre infrastructure that did exist in the south has been destroyed by war and, since 1991, by inter-factional conflict among various ethnic groups and rebel forces.

War-damaged bridge, Rumbek County, Buheirat State

CRISPIN HUGHES/OXFAM

Northern Darfur

Na'am River, Bahr el Ghazal

Early history

Beginnings

So far, archaeologists in Sudan have not found any trace of our earliest forebears, such as the Australopithecenes or other early hominids found at Olduvai George in Kenya and in Ethiopia. Perhaps such evidence still waits to be uncovered in some remote region.

Our earliest evidence for human occupation dates from Palaeolithic times, the Old Stone Age. Before 30,000 BC, hunter gatherers, moving from the south and west, began to establish themselves over wide areas of the north, west, and central regions of Sudan. Their culture flourished for many thousands of years, leaving rich deposits of stone tools scattered across the deserts.

From 10,000 BC, in the Mesolithic (Middle Stone Age) period, people began to settle along river valleys, particularly by the Nile. Slowly, over several millennia, hunting and gathering gave way to agriculture and animal husbandry, and the large-scale production of pottery — all characteristics of the Neolithic (New Stone Age) period. Complex social structures began to develop, as we know from discoveries of funerary goods, jewellery, and imported luxury items.

Around 3000 BC, a deterioration of the climate of the Sahara, some historians believe, may have caused another influx of people, migrating from the west towards the Nile. These new migrants are thought by many to have been ancestors of the Nubians, a people who were to play a significant role in the future of Sudan.

Sudan and Egypt

Egypt, lying to the north of Sudan, and connected to it by the Nile, played a central role in the country's history. By 2300 BC, Egypt had begun to extend its empire southwards into Sudan, following the course of the Nile. Gradually, the Pharaohs of the Middle Kingdom established several military posts along the river.

During the turmoil that marked the end of the Middle Kingdom, Egypt withdrew from Sudan. But from 1580 BC onwards,

Carved effigy near Akot, Rumbek County
CRISPIN HUGHES/OXFAM

11

Sudan was recolonised, the Egyptians now extending their territory to the fourth cataract of the Nile. This was no longer a military occupation, but colonisation: Sudan was an Egyptian province, known as Nubia and ruled by a governor known as 'the Pharaoh's Son'. Exports to Egypt included cattle, ivory, gum arabic, timber, and slaves; Nubia became the primary supplier of gold to the Pharaohs. It also provided a safe route overland to the spicelands of Punt (modern Somalia).

The Kingdoms of Kush

The power of Egypt was overthrown in 725 BC by Kashata, the first of the Kushite kings. Some historians suggest that Kashata and his subjects were not only the distant ancestors of the Nubians of the present day, but that subsequent Pharaohs were also Nubian. 'Tutankhamen', for example, is a concatenation of Nubian words. Kashata established the Napata kingdom, which stretched from Aswan in Upper Egypt to the Blue Nile. His son, Piankhy, completed his father's ambitions, conquering all of Egypt and bringing it under Sudanese rule.

Episcopalian priest in a camp for displaced Dinka people, Eastern Equatoria. He ministers to 12 churches in the area.
Crispin Hughes/Oxfam

The Assyrian invasion of Egypt meant that contact with Egypt was severed, and Napata declined, to be replaced by the Kingdom of Meroe, perhaps the most well-known name in Sudan's earliest history.

Meroe

The Kingdom of Meroe, which lasted from 350 BC to 350 AD, flourished alongside Roman and Hellenistic Egypt. It was through Egypt, particularly through the port of Alexandria, that contact was maintained with the Mediterranean.

The ruins of Meroe, particularly the temple to the god Amon, the royal palaces, the swimming pool, and, perhaps most strikingly of all, the pyramids at Bagrawiya are evidence of a sophisticated civilisation closely in touch with Mediterranean trade and produce, though hardly touched by its art and culture.

With the fall of Meroe to King Azana of the Ethiopian Empire of Aksum, the picture becomes obscure until the rise of the three kingdoms of al-Marris, Onubatia, and al-Maqara.

Christianity and the coming of Islam

Christianity spread from the north, brought first by believers escaping Roman persecution, and then, after Constantine's conversion, by traders, travellers, and missionaries. By the sixth century AD, the Emperor Justinian was sending regular missionaries to Sudan. The three kingdoms converted to the Coptic Church of Constantinople and merged into two: Nubia and Alawa.

In the seventh century AD, the newly formed Egyptian Islamic state invaded Nubia and the north-east of Sudan. The Egyptian forces met strong opposition, and treaties were signed that governed the relationships between Nubia and Egypt for six centuries. There is evidence that Nubian knights fought on the side of the Christian invaders in the Crusades.

However, Muslim culture and trade strongly influenced Nubia, gradually gaining ascendancy there and in southern Kordofan. Islam did not penetrate into the

13

CHRIS PETERS/OXFAM

Sufi dancers outside a
mosque in Khartoum

south, however, probably impeded by the
strong presence of the Dinka and Shilluk
peoples.

In the fifteenth century, the Christian
kingdom of Alawa in the north was taken
over by Muslims. But their control of
Sudan was short-lived. They lost it in 1504
to the Funj, black Africans who probably
came from the east of the country by the
Blue Nile. They established 'The Black
Sultanate', which was to last until 1821,
when it fell to Turco-Egyptian invaders.

The name 'Sudan' derives from *Bilad-as-Sudan*, 'the Country of the Blacks',
a term used by Arab traders in the
Middle Ages to describe an area of
land stretching roughly from the Red
Sea south of the Sahara to the Atlantic
Ocean.

The nation state defined

Turco–Egyptian rule, 1821–1881

Under Turco–Egyptian occupation, the creation of a modern nation state, albeit with deep divisions, began. The country's boundaries were demarcated, more or less as they are today; the equatorial regions of the south were incorporated; and Khartoum was established as the capital city and central authority of the country. The Khedive of Egypt appointed the British army officer, Charles Gordon, to the post of Governor-General of Sudan.

The south of Sudan was now open for the first time to the sustained influence of the north, and trading networks were established. Initially traders sought ivory, but trade in slaves was more lucrative. Slave-trading became the principal *raison d'être* for the foreign administration (although Gordon fought doggedly against it).

The Mahdiya

In 1881, a messianic religious leader known as the Mahdi (Muhammed Ahmad el Mahdi, 'the Rightly Guided One') led the northern tribes in a successful uprising against Turco-Egyptian rule. General Gordon was killed in 1885, when Khartoum was taken by besieging Mahdist forces.

In 1896, to prevent French expansion in the Nile basin, Sudan was invaded by an Anglo-Egyptian army under Sir Herbert Kitchener. In spite of fierce opposition, the Mahdist state was crushed at the battle of Omdurman in 1898.

Anglo–Egyptian rule, 1898–1955

The Anglo–Egyptian Agreement of 1899 established a 'condominium' administration, based in Khartoum. The cultural, social, and economic divisions that already

River boat on the Blue Nile, near Khartoum

JEREMY HARTLEY/OXFAM

existed within Sudan were deepened by a policy of rapid modernisation in central and eastern Sudan, where industry, commerce, and infrastructure were developed.

The Arabic language and Islam provided cohesion for the social and political aspirations in the north, giving a further focus for national unity along the Nile Valley. Economic development was concentrated mainly on irrigation and agricultural schemes in these areas, to the detriment of those areas deemed 'African', which were viewed as less productive or less accessible. In 1922, 'closed areas' were established in the south, in an attempt to control the internal slave trade. Restrictions on work and travel were used in some provinces to control the spread of Muslim influence. By 1930, the south and the north had become more or less totally isolated from each other.

The road to independence

By 1946, the British administration, to prevent Egypt from reasserting its claim to control Sudan, was taking steps to prepare the country for independence. The policy of separate development of north and south was reversed in 1947. But southern Sudanese people lagged far behind many of their northern compatriots in educational attainment, economic development, and any real involvement in the administration of the country, which was largely in the hands of a northern elite.

In 1954, the newly elected Sudanese parliament debated the future of Sudan. Southern representatives argued for the establishment of federated states, to ensure equality of power after independence; but their case was persistently ignored, and they became convinced that they were being used merely to get the British out of Sudan. Their fears were not unfounded, as subsequent events were to prove.

On 1 January 1956, Sudan achieved independence from Anglo-Egyptian rule. However, the legitimacy of the new government to rule Sudan had already been called into question by certain elements within the Sudanese army. In the preceding August, suspicious of the aims of the government-elect, several garrisons of the Equatoria Corps had mutinied in southern Sudan, and captured several towns in the province.

Omen of war: a child's drawing on the wall of a ruined school in Akot

Four generations of conflict

The incurable poison

The army mutiny in the south was put down, and many of those involved fled abroad and formed opposition groups in exile. In Khartoum, successive parliamentary governments proved unstable and powerless to unite the country. In 1958, to halt the drift towards federalism, General Abboud seized power. He abolished parliament and political parties, established military rule, and accelerated the trend towards Arabisation of the structures of civil power. Many former politicians and intellectuals took to the bush or went into exile.

By 1963, the Sudan African National Union (SANU), based in neighbouring Uganda, had become the official party of the rebel forces; an armed wing, *Anya Nya* — The Incurable Poison — was formed. Fighting intensified, and, following a revolution in 1964, General Abboud relinquished power, having failed to find solutions to Sudan's growing economic problems or to the civil war.

A parliamentary government was elected, but armed conflict continued. In this period the splits that were to weaken successive rebel movements began to appear, as personal ambitions exploited ethnic and tribal differences in the

Wounded SPLA soldier in Kongor, south Sudan

CRISPIN HUGHES/OXFAM

scramble for power. However, by 1970 the Southern Sudan Liberation Movement (SSLM) had been formed, uniting most of the factions, including the Anya Nya.

The years of uneasy peace

In 1969 Colonel Mohamed Jaa'far Nimeiri came to power in Khartoum after a military coup; his presidency was to last until 1985.

The civil war was brought to an end in 1972, when Nimeiri and the rebels signed a peace agreement in Addis Ababa which gave limited autonomy to the south. The Addis Ababa Accord, followed by the Regional Self-Government Act, made the provinces of Bahr el Ghazal, Upper Nile, and Equatoria into a self-governing unit, with an elected regional assembly and a High Executive Council (HEC). Anya Nya forces were incorporated into the army.

But between 1980 and 1983, the government breached the Addis Ababa Accord by dissolving the HEC and the regional assemblies, and dividing the south into three regions. Disputes continued over the use of resources and the unbalanced approach to economic development.

The current civil war

In 1983, the Sudan People's Liberation Army and Movement (SPLA/M) was formed under the leadership of a Dinka, Dr John Garang, who sought support from the Mengistu regime in Ethiopia. Gradually the SPLA took control of large areas of the south.

In 1985 Nimeiri was deposed in a popular uprising led by a powerful trade union movement and radical syndicates of the professional classes. This movement was taken over by a coalition of conservative forces who reinstated the established Sudanese political elite. The general election of April 1986 led to three years of civilian rule under Sadiq el Mahdi, until he was deposed in June 1989 by Brigadier (now General) el-Bashir, backed by the National Islamic Front. On seizing power, the new government banned political parties and systematically destroyed the

organised opposition, particularly those elements which had been instrumental in the overthow of Nimeiri.

By 1993, government forces had retaken some of the towns and garrisons previously held by the SPLA, and were attacking and destabilising the rural areas held by the rebels This military success was helped by increasing divisions among the rebel movement.

Differences among the SPLA's commanders came to a head in August 1991, leading to a split into two factions. Fighting between the two dominant groups — SPLA Mainstream, led by Dr Garang, and SPLA United, led by Dr Riek Mashar — has been responsible for the deaths of many civilians and gross abuses of human rights.

Although further fragmentation of both SPLA factions has occurred, Mainstream has emerged as the dominant military opposition to the government. It currently controls much of Western Equatoria and parts of Eastern Equatoria, Lakes, Jonglei, and Upper Nile. The original aim of the SPLA was to establish a secular, unitary State, with diminished powers for central government. More recently, Mainstream has adopted the principle of self-determination for southern Sudan, arguing that southerners should have the opportunity to vote in a referendum on a range of options, including a federal relationship with the north, and complete autonomy.

In September 1994, SPLA United renamed itself the Southern Sudan Independence Movement (SSIM). Based in Upper Nile, and reported to be fragmenting still further, it seems to have lost much of its former power.

Living in the shadow of war

No one knows exactly how many people have died in the current civil war in Sudan. The US Committee for Refugees estimated in 1992 that 1.3 million southerners alone had died as a direct or indirect result of the war since it began in 1983. A further two million were thought to have been displaced from their homes; 90 per cent were estimated to be women and children.

Displaced Sudanese now live mainly in urban areas in the north, but also in parts of the south held by the SPLA and in areas not directly affected by the fighting. Many others, several hundred thousand, are refugees in neighbouring countries such as Uganda and Kenya.

The UN estimated in 1996 that of the estimated five million people living in the south, two million were in need of emergency food aid. The economy of the whole of Sudan, but particularly in the South, is in a state of collapse, and national resources are being squandered on conflict rather than development.

Josephine's story

'I come from Agangrial in Bahr el Ghazal [Buheirat State], where I was a traditional birth attendant in my village. Because of the fighting, a lot of us left our homes and started walking towards the border with Ethiopia [a distance of some 900 km]. It took weeks to get there, and, once in Ethiopia, we were put into a refugee camp. It was not good there, but we got fed and we survived, although there was violence in the camp, and many women were hurt — raped and beaten. I learned from foreign workers there about Western medicine and midwifery, and this helped me to be a better birth attendant.

'In 1991 [the fall of Mengistu], we had to leave Ethiopia and we started walking back to Sudan. It was a long journey and there was a lot of unhappiness and people died. People starved — just died; lots of children were sick and died. Other people were killed in the fighting or raped and attacked. Wild animals also took some people. I remember that there was a lion that attacked people and took them off screaming.

'Eventually, I arrived in Kapoeta [in Eastern Equatoria] and I felt safe, and began practising as a birth attendant, but the fighting happened again. So I left and walked back to Agangrial, my home [a distance of 600 km].'

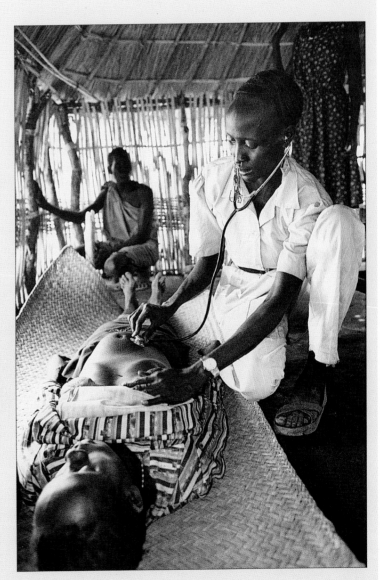

Photo: Crispin Hughes/Oxfam

What is the war about?

It is too simple to present the civil war as a conflict between ideologies of north and south. But it is true that Arabic culture, religion, and language have been the dominant force behind the unification of the north and central regions of Sudan — a process which has exposed and intensified the latent divisions of the country.

During the Condominium, the British employed sectarian policies, including virtual partition of the country, for divisive political ends. In preparation for Independence, the colonial power promoted conservative political parties, which were allied to Britain rather than to Egypt. All governments since Independence, whether elected or not, have professed their intentions of 'Arabising' Sudan to varying degrees, and, in some instances, of creating an Islamic State. In 1983 President Nimeiri imposed *Shar'ia* (Islamic law) throughout Sudan. In 1989, General el-Bashir declared the civil war a *jihad*, or holy war. But many observers would argue that religion, although it cannot be ignored as one cause of the conflict, has been skilfully exploited by those in power, seeking to legitimise the war and unite Muslim opinion behind their actions. Nimeiri, for example, probably acted less from religious conviction than from a need to strengthen his political position.

In fact there has traditionally been a considerable degree of mutual tolerance among Muslims and non-Muslims, and a respect for each other's religion and culture. Tolerance and diversity are fundamental to the culture and values of Sudanese Islam. Muslim society still retains many of its more liberal traditions.

The war between the government and the rebel groups in the south is centrally concerned to define the identity of the Sudanese state, and to establish control over the natural resources of the south. Because of its minerals, its oil reserves, hardwoods, and vast tracts of unexploited lands, control of the south is a key objective for all parties in the current war.

While the government holds the majority of towns in the south, the mainly Dinka SPLA Mainstream controls much of the surrounding countryside. Within the Nuba Mountains is a pocket of the Nuba people, intact under the control of the SPLA (which also holds another remote area of the Ingessena Hills). In Upper Nile State, factions of the mainly Nuer South Sudanese Independence Movement (SSIM) compete with each other for dominance, and the SPLA is attempting to use force to impose unity on them all.

The conflict has caused — mostly in the south, but not entirely so — the near-collapse of traditional economies and mass displacements of people. Drought turned into famine in many of these areas during the 1980s and early 1990s, not least because the conflict has undermined the traditional ways in which different groups of people interact with each other, and their traditional methods of coping with drought, such as gathering wild foods and catching fish.

All sides in the war are guilty of violating the basic human rights of the civilian population. Since 1983, defenceless communities have endured the burning of villages, summary executions, rape, scorched-earth campaigns, indiscriminate bombing, forced displacement of people from their homes, and the military conscription of young boys. The costs of the war — in terms of wasted lives, environmental damage, and lack of economic and social development — are catastrophic.

opposite: Air-raid drill at Palotaka School for war orphans, south Sudan

The bread-basket of the Arab world?

The first large-scale irrigated farming schemes in Sudan were established by the British in El Gezira in the 1920s, to produce cheap cotton for the mills of Lancashire. Covering some 800,000 hectares of land between the Blue and White Niles, the Gezira remains the largest irrigated agricultural scheme in the world. In 1944, mechanised farming began on the fertile lands of eastern Sudan.

After Independence, economic development continued to focus on El Gezira, Kassala, and Khartoum, to the detriment of other areas of the country. Several big schemes were started, including one backed by the Arab Fund for Economic and Social Development (FESD). The FESD plan envisaged Sudanese resources of water, land, and labour combining with Western technical expertise to produce wheat, sugar, animal feed, and meat for export to the Arab world, notably the Gulf.

These projects were over-ambitious and ill-managed. Capital-intensive schemes like this made Sudan even more dependent on imports of oil and machinery, and foreign technology and expertise. Sudan's economy, like that of many other countries on a similar economic path, was crippled by the oil crises of the 1970s; its foreign debt rose dramatically. Fresh inputs of money in the 1970s from Arab investors failed to turn these big schemes into viable enterprises.

In the 1970s, work started in the south on the exploitation of resources, especially oil (first discovered in 1979), minerals, water, and land. A number of development projects were set up. However, the extent to which southerners themselves would benefit was doubtful.

The debt crisis deepens

The Sudanese government, getting deeper and deeper into debt, turned to the International Monetary Fund for help. The IMF prescribed a programme of economic structural adjustment and an emphasis on cotton production rather than wheat. However, as cotton production revived after the drought of 1978, Sudan suffered a second round of oil price rises.

By 1982, oil accounted for 27 per cent of all Sudan's imports; this, combined with escalating interest rates, undermined an already weak economy, and the crisis was compounded by the start of the civil war in 1983.

As a condition of further loans, the IMF demanded reforms which successive Sudanese governments were reluctant to implement, such as the removal of subsidies on basic foodstuffs and the privatisation of utilities and State-owned industries. In 1990, Sudan's membership of the IMF was suspended. However, a

The irony of Sudan's oil

Oil is a major element of Sudan's economy. At present the annual bill for imports of oil and oil-based products is $315 million — which is more than half of the nation's total expenditure on imports. The irony is that Sudan has its own significant deposits of oil, discovered in the early 1980s by the American company Chevron and the French company Total in the south and the west of the country — but they cannot be extracted, because of the war.

Sudan has only one commercially viable oil refinery: at Port Sudan on the Red Sea coast, built by Shell/BP. There is a pipeline to carry the oil from Port Sudan to Khartoum. The government has a 75 per cent stake in the local subsidiary of Total, which markets the oil.

Sudan's oil reserves have been estimated by the World Energy Council at some 200 billion barrels, but no one knows how much of this would be commercially exploitable.

Delivering cotton to the Delta Corporation Cotton Board, Tokar Town

programme aimed at liberalising the economy was finally introduced in 1991. According to some Northern economists, in many cases the main beneficiaries of the privatisation are people closely associated with the government.

By 1995, in spite of continuing condemnation of Sudan by many human-rights organisations and Western governments — most notably the USA — it seemed that the IMF might consider lifting its suspension and reach a deal with the Sudanese government on its proposed economic reform programme.

As a condition of reinstatement to full membership of the IMF, Sudan would have to keep up satisfactory debt repayments for two years. Only then would it be able to negotiate new loans. The government would have to persist with its adjustment policies and thus assure international banks of the country's ability to manage its own economy. It would have to remove government subsidies on almost all consumer goods, privatise still more publicly owned industries and utilities, and increase its tax revenue. How can such a schedule be implemented without causing further hardships to the majority of Sudanese? This question has not, so far, been publicly addressed by either the government or the IMF.

The Jonglei Canal

For many people in the south, the Jonglei Canal project on the flood plains of the Sudd symbolises government attitudes to economic development in the south and to the people who live there.

The 360-km canal, backed by Western technology and investment, was intended to straighten the course of the White Nile, where the river spreads into a swamp that is nearly the size of England. The canal was intended to drain part of the swamp, so that the water wasted by evaporation and seepage would be saved for agriculture downstream in northern Sudan and Egypt. In theory, several million hectares of new land would come under cultivation. It would also completely change the lives of the people of the Sudd. It could damage the ecosystem and micro-climate of the region, and increase the process of desertification over a vast area. Southerners accused the government of planning to steal their resources, and, under repeated attack by the SPLA, the digging of the canal came to a halt in 1984 — like many similar projects.

Of drought and development

The economic policies pursued in Sudan over several decades have delivered prosperity only to a few — and that prosperity has been gained at enormous costs to the country, its peoples, and its environment.

The blame for these policies, however, lies not exclusively with the various Sudanese governments which implemented them, but also with the development organisations and governments which, directly or indirectly, helped to plan and fund them, and hoped to reap their financial benefits. As in many modernisation programmes around the world, the planners paid little attention to the social and environmental impact of their schemes. Ordinary people, particularly those living in rural marginal areas, were regarded as a source of cheap and disposable labour: as a factor in the equation for economic growth, and little else. Environmental concerns were similarly ignored, in a country where much of the land is marginal, the eco-system is delicately balanced, and drought is an ever-present threat.

The cost of biased development policies

The economic policy of Sudan has actively directed investment into some areas, to the detriment of others. So local economies have declined, and more and more people have left their homes to seek work elsewhere. This internal migration to find employment began during the Condominium period. An estimated 500,000 people still seek seasonal work, moving from one irrigated agricultural scheme to another. Many others move permanently, but with little prospect of making a reasonable livelihood and finding security.

Red Sea Hills, 1991

SARAH ERRINGTON/OXFAM

This drift away from rural communities weakens their economic life still further, making them even more vulnerable to the dangers of drought. Even if migrants are lucky enough to find work, they are paid such low wages that they can't send much money back to their families in the home village. Those who cannot find jobs in agriculture tend to drift to urban areas, where they disappear into the ever-expanding shanty towns on the edges of towns and cities.

The years of the half-gourd

Many people in Sudan will tell you that over the last thirty years or so the climate has gradually become drier. No one is sure whether this is part of another long-term climatic change in Sudan, and in Africa as a whole. Certainly drought is not a new phenomenon in Sudan.

In the Islamic year 1306 (1886), just as the Mahdi's successor was consolidating his new state, 'the Six-Year Drought' began. The drought between 1910 and 1917 was dubbed 'the time of the half-gourd', denoting the meagre ration of grain given to large parts of the population. The rains also failed between 1940 and 1945, and again between 1970 and 1973. The latter drought was dubbed simply *Ifza'una*: 'Rescue Us'. The drought of 1984/85 was the worst this century, affecting ten million people. The drought of 1990/91 was almost equally intense. Periods of prolonged, uninterrupted drought give people no chance to recover, and they become increasingly unable to cope.

But Sudan has also experienced many years of good, if erratic, rains in the last fifty years or so. All over the north and in parts of Equatoria, for example, the grain harvest in 1994, helped on by good rains, was a bumper one. In parts of the north, however, such plentiful rains had followed three years of poor rains. The patterns of rainfall remain extremely unpredictable.

Adapting to uncertainty

Across large areas of Sudan, ecosystems are extremely fragile. Over hundreds of years, the people who live there have evolved

Children's feeding centre, Sinkat, 1991　　　SARAH ERRINGTON/OXFAM

lifestyles and strategies that help them to cope with lean times. These strategies seek to minimise the risks involved, rather than to maximise the returns.

In the north, nomadic tribes such as the Kababish Arabs are a good example of how people adapt to the constraints of a harsh environment. Their livelihood is invested in large herds of camels, sheep, and goats, which move seasonally from one area to another so as not to over-graze the land. Some Kababish, because they live in a low-lying area that is seasonally flooded, cultivate food, using different areas from year to year, according to where the rainfall has been heaviest. Again, the objective is to work in sympathy with the environment, not to damage or destroy it.

The relationship between nomads and farmers used to be a vital part of this symbiosis: the farmers providing grain to the nomads, the nomads providing meat and draught animals to the farmers. Prices, although fluctuating with the size of the harvest and the level of rainfall, remained under the control of both groups, and tended to remain stable. But the delicate balance between environment and people has been deteriorating over the decades.

Cash crops: the vicious circle

Traditional methods of cultivation that helped to conserve and regenerate marginal land have gradually been replaced by the intensive farming of cash crops, which involves the clearance of large areas of marginal land in development areas — land which is then farmed beyond its natural capacity.

Instead of rotating crops and leaving areas of marginal land to lie fallow and to regenerate itself, intensive farming destroys the fragile structure of the soil and hastens its erosion. Much of this agriculture is rain-fed, dependent on rainfall for irrigation of the crops. As crop yields go down, more marginal land is cleared to maintain profits, and this land too is depleted of its frail resources.

opposite: Watering goats in Dahant Settlement, Red Sea Hills

Modern farming requires machines and imported resources such as oil and fertilisers, and these too increase production costs. As populations expand, people find that they have less and less good land for their own subsistence needs, and have to clear poorer land if they are to grow crops for their own consumption.

Water: too little, too much

Seasonal wells dictate how long a nomadic or semi-nomadic group stays in one place before moving on to new pastures. In this way, marginal land is not over-grazed or intensively cultivated, but is allowed to regenerate itself. Limited supplies of water also help to control the size of animal herds.

In the 1960s, hundreds of boreholes were drilled by the government in a 'Freedom from Thirst' campaign, funded by Western donors. Nomadic and semi-nomadic groups tended to settle by these boreholes; trees were cut down for firewood, herds increased on the plentiful supply of water, and the land was intensively cultivated over longer and longer periods of time. The increased herds, concentrated in one place, led to over-grazing. Intensive cultivation led to increased soil erosion.

'Freedom from Thirst' was a well-intentioned campaign, but over the years it slowly destroyed much of the natural environment and the people whose livelihoods depended on it. But it was only when a prolonged drought occurred that the full effects of the policy were felt. As the price of livestock fell, grain prices rose, and more animals had to be sold to maintain the community. Livestock were sold off faster than the herds could reproduce, and their owners found themselves bankrupt. With their animal capital gone, and their livelihood and nomadic way of life destroyed, many had no choice but to migrate to the towns.

27

Coping with change in the Red Sea Hills

A Beja village scene

Omeim village is encircled by bare mountains with jagged peaks, the colour of iron ore. The line of Beja tents are perched like the up-turned hulls of ships on a long line of black rock. A few acacia trees, shaved and flattened by the wind, dot the sand dunes. The day-time temperature in this valley can reach 45 degrees. It seems almost a miracle that anyone can actually survive in this desperately harsh place.

The sun is setting in an orange glow behind the mountains. One star appears and the call to prayer can be heard, echoing round the valley. Young men pass by, carrying traditional Beja swords, on their way to the village mosque — a shelter made from dom palm leaves. Every now and again camels pad by, their feet making a soft plop plop noise as they sink into the sand.

A smell of roasting coffee fills the air. To the Beja, coffee is essential and life-sustaining. Even when there is no food, dignity is maintained if there is coffee to offer to guests. It is served in tiny cups, laden with sugar and tinged with ginger. For the Beja, the *jebana* — the traditional clay coffee pot — is a symbol of home.

Drawing water at a well in Dahant Settlement, Red Sea Hills

Once the Beja were a mostly pastoralist people, moving from one seasonal grazing area to another with their herds. Like many other nomadic or semi-nomadic groups, their way of life has become more and more precarious, undermined by prolonged drought. The mainstay of the Beja economy was, traditionally, livestock: mainly camels, but also sheep and goats. Surplus animals could be sold to buy grain, coffee, and sugar from markets in towns such as Tokar. The Beja grew some basic food-stuffs, but subsistence agriculture was always secondary to animal herding.

It was a lifestyle well suited to the harsh environment. The land was protected from over-grazing and over-cultivation by the seasonal movements of people and animals from one area to another. The large tents of the Beja would simply be dismantled and loaded on to camels, and the whole village would be on the move. In times of hardship, such as drought, communities adopted a system called *silif*, in which resources are shared out in the community, particularly to those most vulnerable.

Perhaps because of their nomadic way of life, the Beja have little influence on economic and social policies, either regionally or nationally. Education and health services in the area are very limited, and the Beja find it hard to gain direct entry into wider markets. Despite the problems of nomadic life, however, the Beja population rose rapidly during the 1970s.

The droughts of 1984/85 and 1990/91 revealed just how tenuous their pastoralist way of life had become. As the drought got worse, the Beja could not cope. Their livestock began to die: half of their animals perished in successive droughts. In normal time, livestock can quickly replenish their numbers after drought, but the droughts in north Tokar were prolonged and the herds could not recover, particularly the camels. Malnutrition rapidly increased, particularly among women and children. With the mainstay of their livelihood drastically reduced, the Beja had to look for alternative ways of making a living.

Rising to the challenge of change

Many of the Beja men got work as labourers in Port Sudan or on agricultural schemes in the Tokar Delta; others migrated to Khartoum. But Beja society also adapted to a changing climate in other, more fundamental, ways.

Nomads in north Tokar load their home on to a camel

SARAH ERRINGTON/OXFAM

29

Mohamed Gaffar, a former nomadic herdsman, with his first tomato crop

SARAH ERRINGTON/OXFAM

Most Beja now live in settled communities, and many have returned from towns and cities to their land. Only a few now want to go back to a purely nomadic life. Seasonal migrations do still take place, but rarely with the whole family. The Beja now concentrate on raising goats, because they can withstand long periods of drought better than camels, and their numbers are more quickly replenished. In addition, many families are experimenting with raising chickens.

Village Development Committees have organised communities to take part in group projects such as digging and maintaining wells, burning charcoal, cultivating gardens, building schools, and making ropes and mats. Although the land is poor, and demands a high degree of maintenance and irrigation, subsistence agriculture is rapidly expanding.

Most of the Beja still live on the margins of survival, with no guarantee that they will not go hungry next year. However, new skills are being learned in North Tokar and in parts of Red Sea, and the Beja are adopting new strategies for survival. Just as importantly, they have learned to co-operate through their VDCs and smaller committees, to pool resources and ideas, to organise loans, and to involve a wider range of community members when big decisions are being made.

Beja women find a voice

Women, in particular, have gained from the changes. They now take part in village debates outside the cluster of family tents which are their traditional, and strictly limited, area of authority. They are also receiving a rudimentary education in VDC schools. Custom would not have allowed this in the old days. Some women even make the journey to Port Sudan to sell their mats and handicrafts — another significant change, since men always used to act as the links between women and the world outside.

Women are not, however, full citizens within Beja society, in spite of the improvements in their status and access to a wider world. In times of food scarcity, women and girls are often the last to receive food. Women cannot inherit land or livestock, only the tent and its contents; other assets pass to the husband's nearest male relative.

Control of the body and the mind

In many areas of Sudan, particularly (but not exclusively) in the east, the practice of female genital mutilation (FGM) is viewed as a cultural norm, a rite of passage for every woman. FGM is still practised in many other countries in Africa, among them Ethiopia and Somalia. In northern Sudan, in spite of attempts to ban it, an estimated 89 per cent of women underwent the operation in 1990 — a slight drop from the figure of 96 per cent reported in

1977/78. The latter survey also showed that 78 per cent of the women questioned still claimed to favour the practice.

In Sudan the commonest form of FGM involves the removal of the clitoris (clitoridectomy) and the sewing together of the labia majora (infibulation). The operation is often performed on infants and young girls. It effectively inhibits or prevents ordinary sexual intercourse, and makes childbirth very dangerous indeed: the woman must be cut open before the birth, and the wound is sewn up again afterwards. Where births take place without trained medical supervision, the wound is often held together with thorns — a practice which increases the chances of infection.

Infibulation is illegal in Sudan, although the removal of the clitoris is still permitted. Many midwives and clinics will not perform infibulation, so parents take their daughters to traditional midwives for the operation.

Many women feel that they cannot speak out against this practice, that they will be ostracised for deviating from a tradition that is central to their own cultural identities. On the other hand, they know that it threatens their lives and takes from them their control over their own bodies.

Armat's story

'My name is Armat. I don't know the year that I was born, but it is said that it was in the year of Independence from English rule [1956]. In my childhood, I used to herd the goats. It was very easy and pleasant: all the valleys were full of grass; trees were green and full of different fruits; the animals were fat and healthy.

'In 1971, things began to change, and there was less rain than before. Our animals died and we moved to a village. My husband got work chopping wood, which he sold to a merchant. In 1982, the government came and dug a well in the village and more people settled here. There was drought also in 1984/85, and in 1990. Oil and wheat provided by a foreign agency saved us from sure death.

'Now we have seen many changes in our community. No longer do many of us migrate, though some still do; we are settled. We have had to change. The Village Development Committee has organised things so that the wells are now hygienic and are kept covered; we have also a group garden. My husband still makes charcoal; but my son Ali borrowed *saffi* [a local grass] from the VDC and makes ropes, which he sells. I now make mats of *saffi* which I also sell.

SARAH ERRINGTON/OXFAM

The men have constructed a classroom in which I and my two daughters have started learning basic writing and reading, and they are training in handicrafts. Out hearts' desire is to have a classroom to be a centre for women, so that we can meet and work to gain knowledge, experience, and power.'

(Meize Village, Red Sea State)

An equilibrium destroyed

All over Sudan, networks of exchange and trade, spanning entire regions and beyond, have evolved over centuries. Goods such as grain, salt, and coffee would be traded 'down the line' into remote places, crossing many ethnic boundaries. Access to grazing land and water was a shared right, or one open to negotiation by all sides.

SPLA commander, Western Equatoria: 'I must keep up with technology, so I can control the army.'
CRISPIN HUGHES/OXFAM

Such reciprocal relationships enabled people to trade with one another, to move to where food and water were seasonally available, and to cope with times of drought and food-shortage. Dinka, Nuer, and Mundari agro-pastoralists, for example, have permanent villages where they cultivate sorghum and finger millet during the rainy seasons. Their cattle are corralled nearby and supply milk, vital for children and old people. In the dry season, the men move their cattle up to 50 km away, to graze on the flood-plains of rivers like the Nile.

The herders often cross the territory of other ethnic groups, relying on well-established networks of mutual obligation. There has always been tension in hard times between these different groups, but conflicts were usually resolved by payment of a fine, agreed by the chiefs of the opposing parties. In this way, conflict was regulated within social structures. It was in no one's interest to push antagonism to a stage where it threatened the future existence of either group.

The equilibrium that had been established over centuries between the various ethnic groups in the south of Sudan has been destroyed by the civil war. Local conflicts over resources have escalated into prolonged and bloody fighting, conducted with modern weapons. In 1991, when the SPLA split into different warring factions, traditional tribal tensions were made dramatically worse by the use of modern weapons, and the civilian population suffered grievously.

The stresses caused by the natural disasters of drought, flash floods, and cattle disease were also compounded when armed conflict erupted. Civilians were massacred, whole herds of cattle were stolen, and houses and property were destroyed. Tens of thousands of people in

'I hid in the forest with my six children ...'

In October 1994, the small town of Akot in Buheirat State was attacked by Nuer militia. More than one hundred people, including women and children, were massacred. Thousands of head of cattle were driven off to be sold in the north. Ding Ater Jok took refuge in a village 15 km away.

'When the Nuer came to Akot, I hid in the forest with my six children, and then we went to another village. The Nuer came across the landing place and into the town. I heard many people screaming and there was gunfire, lots of it.

'I was pregnant last year and, even though I had a hoe, I could not plant much sorghum, and the crop has been

CRISPIN HUGHES/OXFAM

very poor with little rain. My husband is dead, and his brother, who has given me two of my children, is not here.'

this area alone starved to death or fled westwards across the Nile, flooding into Bahr el Ghazal and beyond.

'Peace is the priority'

Fierce fighting continued sporadically in 1995 in many parts of the country, both between government forces and the SPLA Mainstream — as in Eastern Equatoria — and between rebel militia factions in many regions of the south. Paradoxically, some of the militia are backed by the government, in an attempt to weaken the opposition.

The hostilities affect everybody: herders are excluded from traditional grazing grounds; people are driven away from good agricultural land and clean wells. Such conflict and insecurity drain people's resources and make them more vulnerable to natural disasters.

However, the impact of conflict and displacement is not limited to those who are directly affected: it also threatens communities in the areas where they move to. In many regions, the migration of displaced people has put severe stresses on relationships between different sections of the same group, as meagre resources are stretched to breaking point.

'You share the food, you finish it, and you starve together'

'It is a tradition that you do not push away people from your home. You share the limited food, you finish it, and you starve together, so the suffering comes to all of you. Before the war started, people were settled: we had no need to move from place to place, no insecurity. We planted sorghum and finger millet last year, but, because we still all feel insecure after the raid on Akot, we did not plant enough. Then the rains were not very good, and the crops have been poor. People will not go off and fish, because of the insecurity. Now people are hungry, they are full of discontent, they no longer abide by the laws. All this is because of the war. Peace is the priority.'
(*Chief Dut Malual, Akot*)

The health of the nation

Health care is a major casualty of a war which is estimated to be costing the Sudanese government hundreds of millions of dollars a year. Most health-care programmes are under-funded and understaffed. Many people live far from hospitals and rely on community health workers — local people trained in basic medical skills — or on local clinics, some of them run by aid organisations.

Services have virtually collapsed in the areas of Sudan directly affected by the war.

The few facilities that do exist are mostly sponsored by international and national agencies. In the displacement camps around Khartoum there are a few clinics, again mainly run by non-governmental organisations (NGOs).

The World Bank estimates that life expectancy at birth in Sudan in 1993 was 53 years. Malaria takes its toll, along with measles, whooping cough, cholera, meningitis, tuberculosis, and Kala-azar (visceral leishmaniasis).

Poor diet and dirty drinking water are major threats to health; malnutrition is endemic in many rural and urban areas. A study by the National Administration for Nutrition, published in 1994, revealed that, for every 1,000 births, 121 children die of malnutrition or related diseases before they reach the age of five. The study did not include the war-torn south.

Medicine in the south: Dr Chol's rounds

Agangrial in Rumbek county, Buheirat State, is a small village of several dozen Dinka houses and cattle camps. In a clearing nearby, a local clinic is under con-struction: large tukuls of wood and thatch that will house the dispensary, the ante-natal clinic, examination rooms, and a small ward. Early each morning a crowd of people wait under an ancient mango tree in the middle of the compound for the surgery to open.

Dr Stephen Chol is a Dinka from the town of Akot in Central Lakes Province. He has returned to his birth-place to lead a small medical team at the referral hospital in the town. This and the one at Billing 60 km to the south are the only hospitals in this large region. Akot hospital was ransacked by Nuer militia in the raid on Akot in October 1994. Dr Stephen was on

Agangrial clinic, Buheirat State
CRISPIN HUGHES/OXFAM

leave in Nairobi with his Nuer wife and their family when the attack happened.

He has travelled to Agangrial by road: a seven-hour journey along winding dusty tracks and the remains of once-graded main roads. He had to pass through check-points manned by soldiers of SPLA Mainstream, who are the *de facto* power around here.

Casualties of war

Traditional healing skills, passed down from generation to generation in certain families, are starting to disappear in the south of Sudan, another casualty of the war. But a few healers still practise their craft, mending broken limbs and cleaning wounds. Like traditional birth attendants, the healers try to work with local people trained in modern medical techniques. This mix of modern and traditional medicine serves to introduce the clinic to people, and gives traditional healers the support they need to continue their art.

Sudan desperately needs a system that tackles not only the effects of disease but its causes as well. For instance, to tackle water-borne diseases the whole cycle must be dealt with, starting with hygiene at the wells, and following up with basic health education such as the importance of

Dr Stephen's story

'All the drugs were looted in the raid on Akot. I'm sure you can see them for sale in some market or other, or they've gone to some militia. It's taking time to restock the pharmacy. Before the raid, the facilities at the hospital were adequate; I've worked in worse conditions, for example, in Upper Nile State.

'I'm the only doctor for miles and miles, and Akot is the only referral hospital in Lakes, apart from the one at Billing. One of our problems is the lack of trained staff. The International Committee of the Red Cross has funded five nurses, but it's not enough. The sheer size of the area is a problem, and the fact that the roads are bad — impassable during the rainy season.

'The daily complaints are mostly stomach problems. Now it's the end of the dry season and water sources are dwindling. People have to drink from the sources where they wash themselves and their animals. So stomach bugs, including bloody diarrhoea and dysentery, are very common.

'TB is on the decline: I had over one hundred patients in Akot and now there are just seven. But there has been an increase in hernias, particularly among young men. I've not known this before. It's probably to do with hunger: there are lots of people here right on the margin, and the stomach muscles grow weak. Malnutrition has its peaks and troughs: by April it will start to bite again, when food gets scarce.

'Our small health team, run by an NGO, is trying to establish a Primary Health-Care Unit which will train local people to run an outreach unit, with ante-natal programmes, and immunisation and supplementary feeding programmes for children, and other preventative services. It's all pretty standard, but most of it is lacking right now.'

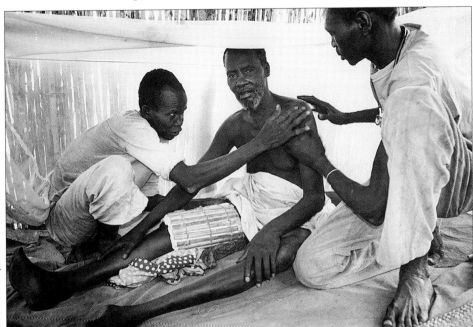

CRISPIN HUGHES/OXFAM

Agangrial clinic: a traditional healer (left) working with a professional health worker (right)

On the outskirts of Omdurman: squalid living conditions pose serious risks to health in resettlement camps

CHRIS PETERS / OXFAM

washing hands – though even soap is hard to get in many areas. If this holistic approach is not adopted, medicine becomes stuck in a cycle of treating the symptoms of disease, not their causes.

Health-care in the north: Dr Ahmed's day

In one of the camps for displaced people on the outskirts of Khartoum, the local clinic is run by Dr Ahmed, two nurses, and several outreach teams. It is one of five such clinics run by an international aid organisation in the camps surrounding Khartoum.

The clinic is housed in a large bamboo compound in the heart of a settlement which stretches for mile after mile in all directions. The clinic is always crowded, with patients milling around outside the dispensary, or sitting patiently on benches in the shade waiting to see a nurse or the doctor.

In his portacabin office, Dr Ahmed examines patients, writes out prescriptions, and oversees the running of the clinic. This one clinic alone treats perhaps 650 people a day, offering supplementary feeding programmes, ante-natal care, immunisation for children, and basic medicines, mainly for malaria and water-borne diseases.

Dr Ahmed's story

'Our outreach workers go out into the camps. In a different area each day, they see perhaps two or three hundred families and their children. They can also assess the general condition of these areas day by day, and note if there are particularly bad outbreaks of malaria or dysentery or malnutrition. The supplementary food for the children is given out to these families once a month. I would like to see many more clinics being opened. Even this one settlement is huge and grows all the time. We're always short of money! And there's never an end to the paper work we have to do.

'But people's health is not just a question of providing more clinics. The environment they live in is also important, and here the lack of work, the squalid living conditions, the broken families, and the malnutrition all undermine people's health.'

I want to learn

All over Sudan, people are obsessed with getting an education for themselves and for their children. People everywhere express a burning wish to learn, to broaden their horizons, and to obtain the skills that will help them to improve their lives.

In the years of peace, primary education was fairly widespread, and a fair number of students managed to go on to higher education in the big towns and outside Sudan, mainly in the Arab world. But in 1992 it was estimated that only 28 per cent of the adult population had basic literacy skills (45 per cent of men, and 13 per cent of women).

In areas of the south where the fighting has died down, however, local teachers working on a voluntary basis are now trying to re-establish schools, and giving language classes in English and Arabic. Many school buildings have been destroyed, so classes are often held under a tree in the centre of the village.

Gordon Kuc, although a modest and retiring man, exudes the air of a person with a definite mission in life. In his case, that mission is to teach, to re-establish education and schools. He speaks English with text-book correctness; although his manner is quiet and unassuming, he carries the conviction of someone who is used to addressing students, and to being heard with respect.

Gordon and his colleagues are slowly beginning to put back together a rudimentary system of education in Buheirat State. It is, as he readily admits, a long process and, like any other initiative, predicated above all else on a sustained peace. He estimates that in some areas directly affected by the war, the literacy rate has declined to 15 per cent for men and 1 per cent for women.

CRISPIN HUGHES / OXFAM

Children playing in the ruins of Akot School — once a large and thriving institution

The right to an education

For girls and women, educational opportunities in Sudan are even more limited than they are for boys. Many ethnic groups are wary of education, if it means exposing women to the outside world, and breaking down cultural traditions that restrict them to the private sphere of the home and family. But many women are beginning to challenge this attitude, by exploiting the opportunities that changing social and economic conditions have created. Women's self-help groups give their members the confidence to claim the right to be educated, and in some areas the bias against them is slowly being redressed; but much remains to be done.

In 1989 a government decree introduced a greater Islamic element into education — a move which is viewed by many observers as restricting still further the educational opportunities of non-Muslim communities.

In some of the displaced people's camps and settlement areas around Khartoum, a few schools provide education for children of different religions. One such school, run by a Catholic mission, teaches about 2,000 children. Such schools are not encouraged by the government, and many do not have official approval.

A teacher in the south

'I am trying to bring in books, blackboards, and chalks. All of the schools were closed or destroyed because of the war, but now because of the stability here — which we seriously hope will last and is essential for everything! — a little primary education and even some secondary education is starting once again. There is now some local organisation, and this helps people working on a voluntary basis to bring education back. We are now trying to pick many things up which were here before the war started, and one day we will expand these things. But we must have peace.'
(Gordon Kuc, Buheirat State)

A teacher in the north

'The parents are mad for education, and it keeps the kids occupied. If they can read and write, they perhaps won't get shoved around so much. As a Catholic priest, of course I have an agenda, but I take them all; whether they are committed Muslims or Christians, or whatever, they all have a God-given right to education.'
(Father Paul, Khartoum)

Narus, Eastern Equatoria: a school for displaced children, established by Bishop Taban and his helpers

CRISPIN HUGHES/OXFAM

Living on the edge of the city

Roughly one quarter of all Sudanese live in towns and cities, but this figure is rising, rapidly and continually, especially around Khartoum.

In the 1960s and 1970s, economic policies in the north left rural areas at a disadvantage. Hunger and exhausted soils in the countryside drove many peasant farmers to seek work in the towns. Khartoum and other conurbations grew ever larger, and so did the demand for cheap, migrant labour in the booming service and construction industries.

Low wages, harsh employment conditions, unemployment, lack of land tenure, and problems in obtaining identity cards were to become the fate of many migrants to the city during the 1970s and 1980s. As the civil war and drought in the mid-1980s increasingly affected the civilian populations of the south and west, urban migration grew dramatically. According to

The brain drain and the urban cash-flow

Many Sudanese professional people live and work outside Sudan, mainly in the Gulf states. The remittances which they send home make a major contribution to the wealth of the big cities, particularly Khartoum, where their cash stimulates land speculation, domestic and commercial construction, and demand for consumer goods.

However, after Sudan's moral support for Iraq in the Gulf War of 1991, relations between Sudan and Saudi Arabia have deteriorated, and many thousands of migrant Sudanese workers were expelled.

Zagalona, an industrial area of Khartoum

JEREMY HARTLEY/OXFAM

the UN, approximately half of Khartoum state's estimated population of 3.6 million consists of displaced and migrant people.

Squatters and displaced people

Squatting was, until quite recently, a long-standing tradition in Khartoum, tolerated because the cities needed a cheap and locally based work force. Much of Khartoum North and Omdurman developed in this way.

Since 1989, it has been government policy to remove squatters from illegal settlements in and around Khartoum and relocate them, either to officially designated camps for the displaced, or (if they can prove that they have lived in Khartoum since before 1990) to new settlement areas, where they are granted land rights.

The government states that the relocations are part of its urban planning exercise, an aspect of the Khartoum Structure Plan of 1989, which was funded by the World Bank. Illegal squatting is viewed as a danger to public health, and the source of serious social and economic problems, all of which threaten neighbouring areas. Magistrates oversee the evictions. Local-authority workmen bulldoze dwellings and load up people on to lorries. Magistrates can authorise the use of force if it is deemed necessary.

The government has the right to remove illegal squatters from land to which they have no legal claim, and to replan Khartoum accordingly. But in the name of urban replanning and renewal, many people are forced to live farther away from sources of employment, in areas without basic services. In some camps, such as Jebel Aulia, 40 km south of Khartoum, basic services such as water supplies and subsidised public transport have, over time, been put in, but they are still inadequate. Insecurity pervades life for everyone in these communities.

By the end of 1991, tens of thousands of people had been relocated to temporary camps. By 1992, some 700,000 people had been removed from the capital. Between August 1993 and July 1994, a further 160,000 dwellings were demolished.

Thowra, Block D Settlement, Omdurman

The *tukuls* of the residents — tents made of plastic sheeting, bamboo, mud brick, and sacking — stretch for miles across the bare desert. Children play around them, or sit with their parents in the shade looking out at the desert. A few women are hanging out washing, while a group of men are busy digging out rough mud building bricks from the earth. A few dogs and goats wander around, looking for food.

There is little litter, not even the ubiquitous plastic bags that cover much of the waste ground of the city. The noise and bustle which are the hallmark of many urban slums throughout the world are largely absent. Thowra is cut off from the networks of services, investment, and opportunities that are vital for any settlement to prosper. Thowra has no health clinics, schools, or shops, and there is little chance of finding work. Water is bought from a water seller or from the nearest small market, 2 km away.

Sitting on a camp bed inside her tukul of bamboo and plastic sheeting is Faith (not her real name). Faith is in her late thirties, a large, homely woman, and the mother of ten children. In spite of the story she relates and the bleakness of her surroundings, she has a quiet dignity, punctuating her speech with thanks for the small mercies that life has given to her, her husband, and children: she knows many families who are far worse off than themselves.

'In the city, you can feel your poverty.'
(Street girl, Khartoum)

Faith's story

'I am from Kordofan and I have been here since 1970. We came here to Khartoum to look for work. But, although we found work, we had no security for our plot ... We were moved out by force in the night and there was much fighting. They took everything — all our possessions. They pushed over my house to make way for a private development scheme. Here, in Thowra, we have nothing.

'The bamboo and plastic for our tukuls was given by a charity, and woollens for the children, and water containers. Without this we had nothing. We were taken here and dumped off by a truck in the night. Some people had to walk. It was very cold, and we were all very frightened. The children felt the cold very badly. We had no shelter and just sat in the sand.

'The other place from where we were moved [El Khuddair] had a school, and the Sudan Council of Churches was working with us on handicrafts (although we sold very few of the things), and there was some teaching for my children. Here, there is nothing. If the children get sick, there is a traditional healer, but there is no doctor or clinic. Water is expensive, but there is no alternative: money must be found. For if you do not have money, you do not get water.

'There is little chance of getting work, but we are lucky: my husband kept his job as a watchman in Khartoum. I have ten children. Most of my neighbours do not have work. We have nothing to sell, and no one but people like you or the authorities ever comes here. It is a long way [20 km] to the centre, where we might get work. But with a bit of money and raw materials, we could make more money. Do I want to go back home? Some people do, but I will stay here. I have been away from Kordofan for over twenty years.'

LIBA TAYLOR/OXFAM

Making ends meet in the city

The cities are hostile places for migrants and displaced people, who arrive from the countryside with little education and few skills to enable them to survive in town. 'Formal' employment is virtually impossible to obtain; for those who do find regular jobs, as guards or office cleaners, the slack labour market means rock-bottom wages.

The 'informal' sector

Most poor people in Khartoum and towns and cities throughout Sudan try to find work within the 'informal' sector: work that is not covered by labour laws, requires no formal education, is untaxed, non-unionised, and poorly paid.

A high proportion of the displaced are women and children; many of the women are the sole source of support for their households. They mostly get work cleaning, washing clothes, and selling tea, vegetables, and kitchen utensils. But in some camps and settlements, brewing beer and prostitution are the only ways in which women can stay alive. Men make a living by selling tea and other items such as cigarettes and water, by washing cars, and, for those who have a trade, by carpentry and plumbing. Many men, especially those who have recently arrived in the city, or have been forcibly removed from established communities, get occasional work as unskilled labourers on agricultural and construction projects.

Although most of the poor and displaced in Khartoum struggle to make ends meet, a very small number not only find work, but form small co-operatives. Helped by voluntary organisations and church groups, they have found a precarious niche in the labour market, and also a degree of autonomy and control over their own lives.

The brick makers

The practice of making mud bricks from alluvial mud laid down each year by the Nile has been going on for thousands of years. It is seasonal work, which stops for three months when the Nile floods in August. The bricks are made from a mixture of mud, straw, and donkey manure. The mixture is pushed into wooden brick moulds, from where the bricks are removed to dry in the hot sun, before being baked in large mud-lined kilns.

Most of the small brick-making companies that work the rich, dark Nile mud are privately owned; the employees have few rights and little pay. In 1993, a small number of brick makers, all of them living on the fringes of Khartoum, got together and joined a craftsmen's union, thus enabling them to start their own brick-making co-operative.

The tea and vegetable sellers

Markets in Khartoum are sprawling, bustling, open-air affairs, full of colour, noise and activity. As panel beaters knock the dents out of bumpers, carpenters assemble beds, and a scrap-yard busily recycles yards of rusty wire and metal piping, shopkeepers and stallholders drum up trade. Buses crash their gears and hoot their horns as they weave between hand-drawn carts and bicycles and the crowds of shoppers who dart across the roads.

In one small corner of one such market, opposite a car-repair shop, a group of women sit beneath a metal awning, making tea. The market is hot and dusty, and the women, protected by their awning from the harsh sun beating down from a deep blue, cloudless sky, are doing a brisk trade in selling glasses of sweet tea.

'I come from a squatter settlement called Mayo Farm. I am the only one working in my family. I used to work as a brick maker for a private firm, but now I am with the co-operative. I am skilled at my trade and that is why I got this job. I had to pay 5,000 Sudanese pounds as a registration fee. The profit is split according to what each person does, after we have taken the running costs out; each man works for himself, but no one man owns our company. We have 93 men in the co-operative.'

Nearby, a mud-brick building which will house five tea shops, a storeroom, and an office nears completion. The women, members of a co-operative, all own a share in this latest venture and are looking forward to moving into their new accommodation.

A local group, the Sudan Development Agency (SDA), run mainly by Sudanese women, was the guiding force behind the establishment of this co-operative of tea and vegetable sellers, offering legal advice, moral support, and the initial funds to set up a co-operative bank.

The co-operative has 24 members. They have obtained official trading permits and built shelters, and are now building the small complex of shops and offices nearby — their most ambitious venture. Through SDA, a committee of six women was formed, to be responsible for lending money to members, to help pay for shelters, and to buy tea and utensils. As one loan is paid back, another woman can borrow money to set herself up. The interest on this money is used to build the centre and to provide hardship funds to members who are sick or unable to work.

Through the co-operative the traders have gained legal recognition, and a degree of security from abuse by established stallholders.

A tea seller's story

'My name is Fatima. I live in Jebel Aulia settlement with my two children and my husband, who is unemployed. I belong to the SDA co-operative, and I run a stall next to other members' stands in one of the biggest markets in Khartoum.

'I am the only one in my family who is working. I used to get into trouble working in the market trying to sell tea, especially with the police. You see, men don't like women to work like this; it is not a proper thing for women to do.

'But now things are changed. I had a medical examination and then I was issued with a permit to trade by the authorities. I am in a good place to work, shaded from the sun. The SDA has given me confidence and skills. We buy tea in bulk, and have learnt how to keep an account of what we sell. Most of all, we are learning that we have strength by being women together. Because we were not organised before, we had no strength.'

Making ends meet in the countryside

Trade and markets are the lifeblood of any society. In many parts of southern Sudan, commercial activity has collapsed because of the civil war. This situation is made worse by the lack of all-weather roads: most roads are dirt tracks cut into the forest and savannah, and, even before the war, travelling in areas of high rainfall was impossible for much of the year.

Trade with the north of Sudan via Northern Bahr el Ghazal was disrupted by fighting between Dinka and Baggara people in Southern Darfur and is only slowly recovering. Trade with the north via the Nile came to a complete halt years ago. The towns, which previously gave people a place to sell cattle for grain or for other necessary things, have largely been destroyed and are no more than military garrisons for the government, cut off from the rural population. Roads into Uganda and Zaire have been closed by the Sudanese government in an attempt to block the SPLA's supply routes. Only a trickle of goods can be brought into southern Sudan by bicycle convoys, which take back paths across the borders, bringing in used clothes and other small items.

Two markets in the south

In spite of these problems, a few markets do survive in some form or other, even though the countryside is still insecure and there is little to trade. For a market is more than a meeting place for trade: it acts as a focus for people, where information, gossip, and news can be exchanged, and a sense of security regained, if only for a short while.

Although bartering is widespread, a cash economy does exist in a limited way. Use of the Sudanese pound has helped to set agreed prices and stabilise the limited local economy. In these self-styled 'New Sudan' territories, the newly formed National Executive Council — under the supervision of SPLA Mainstream — is trying to set up a local civil administration; but it has few resources and the countryside is still largely insecure, so power is still overwhelmingly in the hands of the armed wing of the movement.

In parts of Western Equatoria and Buheirat State, markets are held regularly. The produce on sale, its quantity and diversity, is a good indicator of the degree to which different local economies — and trade networks farther afield — have been exposed to war and are able to cope. We can see this by looking at two different markets.

A market in the bush

In Buheirat State, markets like the one held every afternoon except Sunday in Bar Pakeng, 40 km west of Akot, reflect the local Dinka economy, which is based on livestock. The market is set in a large clearing in the bush, several hundred metres across. A large area is devoted to cattle sales in one corner of the market.

The selling of cattle is a serious business in any pastoralist society, and the cattle on sale here are carefully scrutinised by prospective buyers. Sellers are cross-examined at length. The transactions are eagerly followed by a crowd of spectators who offer loud advice and opinions, or sagely decline to comment.

The market is a hubbub of activity that draws people from far and wide — a sign that they feel a degree of security returning to their lives: in the past, markets have often been a target for attacks. But what strikes even the most casual observer is that, among the cattle sales, the rows of

Cattle market,
Bar Pakeng

bright print frocks flapping in the strong wind, the knitted hats, and the stalls of looted drugs (for both humans and animals), there is little food for sale — no sorghum and finger millet, no salt or sugar. Small mounds of peanuts and hot chilies and a wild salad vegetable are all the surplus food that is for sale.

Tobacco — a much-prized commodity — is in plentiful supply, often bought when there are no staple foods available, or as an item for future barter. But most people want to buy food, as their own harvests have been so meagre. Despite receiving hoes and seeds from an international agency, farmers did not sow crops in their usual quantity: better not to use all one's seed in one planting, but to conserve some for the uncertain times that might lie ahead. Poor rains have reduced the harvest still further, and what there is must be shared with Dinka people displaced from the east and from farther north.

Perhaps the situation will improve when fish, caught in Lake Nyubor, become available, but the drought may have depleted the fish stocks, and there is also the threat of attack from hostile militia forces on the 60 km trip to the lake.

A market in a town

Some 400 km south of the market in Bar Pakeng lies the little market town of Maridi, in Yei county, Western Equatoria. Close to the Zairean border, the countryside here consists of rolling hills and lush vegetation. This part of the region has not suffered the prolonged fighting that has devastated other areas in the south, and for two years it has known relative peace. The sorghum harvest was exceptionally good in 1995, and there is a surplus.

The local people are not Dinka; they are farmers, members of groups such as the Zande and Moru. Forty kilometres to the south of the town, Dinka displaced by the fighting have built tukuls in the wooded hills. Because of the slowly improving conditions, many have decided to leave and return to their homes in Bor County on the east bank of the Nile; of the 20,000 who once sought refuge here, only some 7,000 remain.

In the walled market in the centre of Maridi, one of few towns under SPLA control, the ground is covered with displays of vegetables, cooking oil (marked 'For Humanitarian Use Only'), drugs, salt, sugar, coffee, grain and tobacco. The market is lined with booths selling soap, clothes, pencils, exercise books, and dresses, all traded up from Uganda. The local economy in Maridi is slowly pulling itself back together: the land is fertile and the rains have been good.

In Maridi, as in other places where a modicum of peace exists, dozens of co-operatives have begun to re-form and go into operation. Co-operatives started here in 1956, primarily to offer local producers a means of breaking the monopoly held by traders, mainly in Juba, the state capital of Bahr el Jabal. Now, throughout the county as a whole, there are over 80 co-ops. But this stability remains fragile and many other parts of the region are still insecure. Trading surplus food out into areas that still suffer shortages is difficult, if not impossible.

The hat seller

'Most of us are widows, so we came together to make these hats. The wool was traded from across the border. We learned how to make hats from mats used to cover food. There are 32 women in this co-operative. Sometimes we sell nothing for three or four days, then we sell one or two for 500 Sudanese pounds.'

The clothes seller

'I buy clothes in bundles in Uganda, or rather we barter for the clothes with bulls: one bull will exchange for a bundle of one hundred dresses. These we sell at 900 Sudanese pounds each, one or two a day. That money is then turned back into buying more cattle. We drive them to the Ugandan border, and the whole trade is started once again.'

Ayen Mawai goes fishing

In Western Equatoria, when the rains are poor, rivers dwindle to muddy pools. Yet not many miles away, heavy rain means deep-flowing rivers and plentiful fish stocks. People trek long distances, despite the risk of attack, to camp under mango and mahogany trees and go fishing.

Keeping the cupboard full

Fish are valued by agro-pastoralists, because they complement grains like sorghum and finger millet and serve as a source of food between harvests.

With many hungry mouths to feed, such a precious resource could quickly become depleted. Being good husbanders of every natural resource available to them, local people are well aware of the need to maintain their fish stocks, and have developed a simple but effective way of replenishing them. For up to fifteen years no one is allowed to fish in certain parts of the river, by order of the local chief. Then, when the chief sees that his people are hungry, or when he is petitioned by the elders of a village, he will order the sacrifice of a ram or a cow, to signify that the ban is lifted and fishing can commence.

In one bend of the river Gel, where fishing has been banned for a number of years, the fish are packed tightly together, churning the waters into a creamy froth. Fishing will go on until this stretch of the river is completely fished out, and then the prohibition will once again be applied for many years to come.

A day's fishing

Ayen Mawai, a young girl from a nearby village, spends much of her day fishing or walking from one stretch of the river to another, carrying her woven, conical

fishing basket on her head. The basket is not heavy and it provides some shelter from the fierce sun as she tramps across the dry, open savannah to reach a stretch of river to fish.

It is a simple matter to know where this is: one just follows the crowd. For fishing here is not a solitary pursuit, but a noisy social event. Along the river bank, dozens of people are gathered, either to fish, or to provide vocal support for those already fishing. Ayen wades into the river to join a ragged line of other women who slowly move forward together, their baskets poised over the water. Every few metres, a woman will drop her basket, trapping a fish inside. It is a simple matter to put a hand into the basket and draw out a wriggling fish, which is then threaded on to a stick.

While Ayen concentrates on her task, boys and girls with pointed sticks walk along the shallows on either side, busily spear-fishing. A little farther upstream, men work in pairs, holding an oblong net stretched between two wooden poles beneath the water. A quick jerk, and the net resurfaces with a couple of fish flopping in the mesh.

'Some days I get a lot of fish; on other days, not so many; it is never enough to feed all the family. It's hard work, but I don't mind it.'

49

Of vets and paravets

Livestock play a crucial part in Sudanese society. By 1992, a combination of war, drought, and displacement had destroyed an estimated 6.6 million cattle in the south, along with 2 million sheep and 1.5 million goats. Such huge losses threatened the disintegration of agro-pastoralist societies in many areas.

Dinka society, like that of the Nuer and the Mundari, revolves around cattle. Local languages have a rich vocabulary to describe cattle in their infinite variety. The camps where cattle are corralled in the dry season are the focal point for pastoralists' social life.

All pastoralist and nomadic groups have a well-developed understanding of the diseases which afflict their animals, and they have devised treatments for each disease. Traditional treatments take account of the spiritual causes of an illness, and rely on the use of certain herbs and the practice of bleeding sick animals. Much of this traditional local expertise is dying out, partly because the civil war has disrupted normal life, and also because modern drugs are so powerful that people lose faith in their traditional skills.

The paravets

In response to these problems, a scheme was devised in the mid-1980s in and around the town of Juba, with the help of a foreign agency. The scheme had two aims: to maintain the traditional veterinary skills of displaced Mundari pastoralists, and to augment their local knowledge with modern veterinary practices. Respected local people are chosen by their communities to be trained to diagnose animal diseases and to run vaccination programmes.

Similar 'paravet' training schemes are now an integral part of many projects and co-operative schemes. Funded by external agencies, programmes are running in North Tokar, Kebkabiya and Renk, Upper Nile, Equatoria, and parts of Bahr el Ghazal.

When displaced people lose their herds of cattle or camels, it is often more realistic for them to restock with sheep, goats, and chickens. Because women are usually responsible for raising these smaller

Mundari paravet in Terekeka District, north of Juba

JON BENNETT/OXFAM

animals, they too have become involved in the paravet programmes. The training increases their skills and raises their status within the community.

A reciprocal arrangement

Giving development aid to poor countries like Sudan is a far from simple matter. For one thing, immense areas have to be covered; communications are bad, and funds are limited. For another thing, the material hand-outs often associated with development aid can undermine local customs and structures, which are already under threat.

Livestock-support projects at first tended simply to give out drugs. But not only did this system undermine the way in which Sudanese societies work, but the projects became a bottomless pit into which expensive drugs were poured. Recently, veterinary programmes have changed their tactics and are setting up revolving funds: a cost-recovery system whereby the paravets obtain veterinary drugs from a central source, and sell them at a fixed and affordable price to livestock-owners. The paravets return the cash to the central office, and receive 20 per cent (in soap and salt) as payment. The rest of the money is spent on community projects, such as building clinics.

This system is beginning to spread throughout much of southern Sudan, working on principles agreed upon by all concerned in the venture. Although it is still in its infancy, this scheme is helping to recreate a market economy and the networks that support it. It is hoped that eventually private traders from Kenya and Uganda will bring in drugs, which paravets can purchase. Of course, it will not be easy. How, for example, can fledgling local authorities effectively police this market and enforce codes of practice, and what role can the chiefs and sub-chiefs play in this scheme? One way forward is perhaps through the setting up of herders' associations; but an animal-health service that enforces codes of practice, regulates prices, and has a sufficient number of trained vets and other staff is still a long way off.

CRISPIN HUGHES/OXFAM

Muslima Mubarak Salih, teaching veterinary skills to other Rasheida women: 'The men selected me for training, because I am permanent here; they move around. I was the first woman paravet.'

SARAH ERRINGTON/OXFAM

Co-ops — Kebkabiya-style

In Northern Darfur, local people in Kebkabiya District, like many other Sudanese communities, have formed themselves into co-operatives.

The town is set in the foothills of the Jebel Marra, and is the administrative centre for the district. This area suffered greatly in the 1980s from drought, famine, and tribal conflict. The region as a whole is under-developed and marginal to the national economy. Many different ethnic groups live here; the Fur are the most numerous.

Along seasonal watercourses, enriched each year by flooding, farmers grow a variety of crops. But people without access to this *wadi* land have to farm the fragile soils away from the river, where erosion and desertification are constant threats. This type of farming depends entirely on rainfall. The chances of rain are increased by the presence of the nearby mountains,

elevating clouds over the land. When it rains, the pastures are green and crops are abundant; but in prolonged periods without rainfall, there is severe stress for people and animals.

Seeding the soil

In 1985, committees were appointed in each village to set up seed banks. From these facilities, farmers borrow not money but seed; after the harvest, they repay the seed, plus a bit extra, so that the bank can lend to other farmers. Certain villagers were chosen to be bankers of the seed.

Despite daunting problems, the scheme began to work. Then villagers successfully experimented with contour farming — ploughing along the contours of the land, to stop rain water draining off the slope. Sixteen Village Centre Committees (VCCs) were formed, and one man and one woman from each village were chosen to

Foothills of the Jebel Marra, Northern Darfur

OXFAM

52

Community veterinary pharmacy, Kebkabiya

represent their community on the Project Management Committee (PMC). Although women initially preferred to form their own committees and exclude men, many VCCs have since reunited, with spin-off sub-committees for women. Other projects were launched, such as training for men and women in basic veterinary skills, along with midwifery classes for women, and literacy and health education classes.

'We know that we have to stand up for our rights if we are to secure them. Although there is a fifty-fifty representation of men and women on the village sugar committee, for example, the men still try to exclude the women from the actual distribution, so that they can keep for themselves the extra amount which is allocated as an incentive for this task. We're working on this problem!'
(Daughter of a village Sheikh, Kebkabiya)

'The post of the village representative to the committees in Segering district had been vacant for some time after the death of the previous member, when I was asked to take it. I was appointed at a general meeting of the village. There was no election and I was the only nominee. I don't know exactly why they chose me, but I've lived in the village all my life and used to be on the Rural Council too, so I suppose that had something to do with it.

'I know that the consultation process is essential to the working of the project and ensures that it meets the real needs of local people. I'm responsible for attending the PMC meetings four times a year and for raising requests at those meetings. After the meetings, I tour the villages and meet with their two representatives, to make sure they know what's happening in the area and to get any feedback from them.'
(Adam Sayed, Segering)

53

A registered charity

Conscious of the fact that the VCCs were new structures which aimed to get better access to resources — and control of them — the people involved were careful to work closely with traditional authorities and with local government, the Salvation Committees. Without the support of these bodies, the VCCs and the PMC could not operate.

As time went by, the PMC was formalised by the creation of the Kebkabiya Smallholders Charitable Society (KSCS), which was registered with the Ministry of Social Welfare as a voluntary organisation at the end of 1990. Official registration meant that the KSCS could raise funds, hold its own budgets, and employ its own staff. An Executive Committee of eleven people from the PMC has been elected to decide and implement overall policy. This Committee meets every three months and is itself accountable for its actions at an annual general meeting of all the Village Committees.

The learning process

Despite the fact that the structure of KSCS promotes accountability and equality between women and men, there are still problems. Some members do not perform their jobs well, while others seek to take advantage of the opportunities which committee membership offers. It is not always easy to 'deselect' such people!

Somati village, Northern Darfur: women's meeting to discuss the introduction of grinding mills
PETER STRACHAN/OXFAM

'Our representative was hopeless. Our village was not getting its share of resources, and we gradually realised that she was not doing anything to find out about it and to tell us. It is true that this went on for years, but that is how things are in the villages: we don't expect things to happen quickly ... Once we realised the true source of the problem, we got rid of her and elected a replacement.'
(Woman from Bora Village)

Nor is it easy for women to get involved in the work of the committees. For one thing, most speak little Arabic — the language in which meetings and correspondence with the Salvation Committees are conducted. For another thing, their household and family duties leave them little time for community work. Traditionally women have not been expected to take part in public affairs; but once they start to speak out, and gain more experience and confidence, they realise they have a voice that is valid and that they can change things. Committee work is the first practical step on the road to empowerment for women.

Will it work?

Although some people still feel that they have not gained much from the KSCS and its committee structure, many others appreciate that learning to manage such a big and complex project takes time. The KSCS offers each member of the community a chance to speak and the skills to change things. Whether it will prove sustainable depends on whether enough of them are convinced that only by becoming involved in community action can they gain control over their own lives.

A marginalised majority

All over Sudan there are countless development initiatives like the Kebkabiya Smallholders Charitable Society. But there is little hope that any of them will prosper without peace and reconciliation and social justice, and a more equitable distribution of economic wealth. Development needs peace, if by development we mean an advancement of the basic rights which every human being is heir to, and not just the powerful few.

In Sudan, as elsewhere, many women still accept inequality as a natural part of their lives. Yet, as we have seen, they are often the mainstay of their societies and a major focus for their regeneration. In times of conflict, displacement, and hardship, the contribution of women to the survival of their families and communities becomes even more critical. The challenges they face often lead them to adopt new strategies to survive, and to ask fundamental questions about the society they live in.

The changing status of women has also affected men. Although some still view women as subordinate and peripheral to the man's world they inhabit, many others appreciate the crucial role that women play in keeping communities together, and they understand the need for change.

Women's literacy class, Gabol Settlement, Red Sea Hills

Nevertheless, the empowerment of women is still a long and uphill struggle, and, if peace does eventually come to Sudan, it will be difficult to maintain the advances made in the economic, social, and political status of women.

Women for peace

There is now a growing movement both inside and outside Sudan to link Sudanese women's non-governmental groups into a wider political process. One such is the Sudan Women's Voice for Peace (SWVP), based in Nairobi, a loose alliance of women from different ethnic backgrounds who see the establishment of women's rights as an integral aspect of the work for peace.

In February 1995, women from the SWVP took a Peace Caravan to parts of southern Sudan, drawing large crowds and generating intense local interest. Their message was in essence a simple one: the absolute necessity for peace and for women to take their rightful role in making that peace a reality.

At the UN conference of women in Beijing in August 1995, the SWVP, along with many other Sudanese groups representing women from different political and cultural backgrounds, met to express their vision of women's future role. The Beijing conference enabled women, and men, to meet other non-governmental organisations and to form new alliances based on a common theme: furthering women's emancipation.

'We women should stand up and work for peace. All the women of Sudan are prevented from influencing political decisions, but we are also the first victims of this most evil war. It is up to us to stop it and, in so doing, to establish ourselves as having a real voice in Sudan and its future.'
(SWVP leader)

A nation in the balance

Both inside and outside Sudan there are informal groups and organisations working for peace. Many others, including highly qualified professional people, work in the service of poor communities to help them cope with the effects of conflict, an impoverished economy, and a rapidly changing environment. But despite this, the efforts of poor people in Sudan to achieve genuine lasting development have borne little fruit. This final chapter looks first at the humanitarian work in Sudan designed to support these people.

Operation Lifeline Sudan (OLS)

In 1989 a three-way agreement was reached between the government of Sudan, the rebel SPLA, and the UN. This agreement created a framework which allowed relief supplies to be delivered inside the war zones to victims of the conflict. This arrangement, whereby a sovereign government permitted the delivery of relief to areas controlled by rebels, was almost unique in the field of humanitarian operations. Currently, OLS operations are run partly from Khartoum and partly from Kenya, with a logistics base on the Kenyan-Sudanese border at Lokichokio. The UN, with UNICEF acting as lead agency, provides logistic and technical support for UN agencies and NGOs working under its umbrella. This is particularly important in the rebel-held areas, where often the only means of access is by aircraft.

But the work of the agencies operating under OLS goes beyond concern with immediate survival. Where possible, they work with local communities to rebuild or strengthen their societies, helping them to coping with the effects of conflict.

Without peace and a secure environment, however, this objective has proved difficult to realise in many areas. Some agencies have to operate as and where they can, mindful that their work could easily be disrupted or stopped altogether by renewed fighting or banditry.

Taposa women in Narus, Eastern Equatoria, a village which has taken in an influx of Dinka people, displaced by the civil war
CRISPIN HUGHES/OXFAM

A dilemma for humanitarian agencies

In conflicts such as the civil war in Sudan, the control of relief supplies can become a strategic asset for the forces involved. In Sudan the relief system has been used in this way by all parties to the conflict. Anti-government forces have treated humanitarian aid, particularly food aid, as a resource for their own troops. In the past, militias adopted a policy of forcibly moving civilians to a particular location where an attack was expected, in the expectation of international assistance. There have also been cases of the direct theft of supplies from humanitarian agencies. For its part, the government has for military reasons denied relief agencies access to certain areas controlled by the SPLA.

There is still an immense need for aid and basic resources. In many parts of the south, relief agencies are the sole source of items such as soap, clothing, and buckets. But the agencies delivering aid, health care, education, and skills training cannot do so without accepting the dictates of one side or another. Thus they expose themselves to the charge that their work is not impartial. More seriously, the international agencies have on occasions been accused of actually prolonging the conflict by indirectly sustaining combatants. Operational agencies must try to satisfy the demands of the government, the UN, the donors, and those in *de facto* control on the ground, while trying to meet the needs of local people.

Of particular concern to the humanitarian agencies is the plight of the Nuba people in Southern Kordofan. Human-rights organisations have documented violations of human rights in the Nuba mountains. Although the government has refuted these accusations, international concern about the situation of the Nuba will remain until unrestricted access is allowed to independent monitors. The Nuba mountains are one of the few areas of conflict excluded from the OLS agreement. Unless the terms of the agreement are extended to include this area, the future of the Nuba people will remain precarious in the extreme.

It is undeniable that, without external support for OLS and the work of NGOs inside Sudan, the suffering of many thousands of Sudanese affected by the war would have been intolerable. Although this suffering has rarely been given front-page coverage by the international media,

OLS air-drop of emergency food supplies in south Sudan

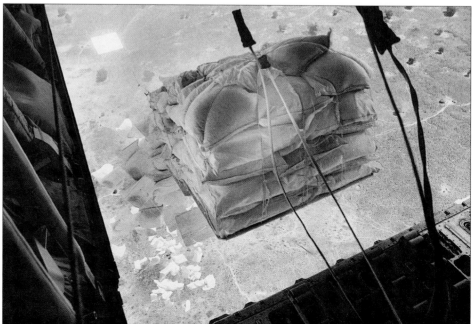

the need for humanitarian aid remains as pressing as ever. To fund its relief operations in support of 4.5 million people in 1996, OLS appealed to international donors for more than $100 million. Judged by the slow response to this appeal, the future of humanitarian aid in Sudan looks perilously insecure.

The quest for peace

A major African peace initiative began in 1993 under the auspices of the Inter-Governmental Agency for Drought and Development (IGADD). It involves several of the countries bordering Sudan: Kenya, Uganda, Ethiopia, and Eritrea. They are concerned to promote peace in Sudan, partly to end the continuing influx of refugees into their countries, and partly to stop a war which has the potential to destabilise much of the region. Although IGADD provides a useful forum for all sides concerned in the conflict, it has yet to achieve a real breakthrough.

There have been other attempts to promote dialogue and understanding among the different parties to the conflict. In 1995, for example, UNESCO hosted a conference in Barcelona, which brought together representatives of government and rebel factions to achieve agreement on a six-point declaration of principles.

But the progress of IGADD and other initiatives has been hampered by a deterioration of relations between Sudan and other IGADD member states. Tensions have arisen along the borders with both Eritrea and Ethiopia; and Sudan and Uganda in 1995 accused each other of armed incursions into their sovereign territories. The conflict in Sudan has also been discussed by the Organisation of African Unity (OAU) over the years. But any peace process in Sudan is unlikely to succeed without better relations between Sudan and its IGADD neighbours.

The fortunes of the war in south Sudan change constantly. The occasional gains made by one side or the other, and the political machinations of government and opposition, pale against the reality that this war is unwinnable by any side. It can only come to an end when all parties agree to lay aside their arms and negotiate a lasting political settlement. Meanwhile, the civilian population will continue to be harassed, looted, displaced, bombed, and shot. The international community can assist in the peace process, but the primary obligation to stop the fighting lies with the government and those who actively oppose it. It remains to be seen whether they have the political will to achieve the lasting peace that countless Sudanese dream of and work towards.

A health worker at Akot Hospital CRISPIN HUGHES/OXFAM

Dates and events

639   Arab Muslims invade Egypt, leading to Sudan's gradual Islamisation

1504 Founding of the Funj Sultanate

1821 Turco-Eygyptian invasion of central and northern Sudan

1881 Emergence of Mahdi as religious leader, opposed to Turco-Egyptian rule

1885 Siege of Khartoum ends with death of General Gordon, leader of Egyptian forces. Mahdist state founded

A typical Dinka house near Akot

CRISPIN HUGHES/OXFAM

1898 Defeat of Mahdist forces by Sir Herbert Kitchener at Omdurman

1899 Establishment of Anglo-Egyptian 'Condominium' to run Sudan

1920s Closed districts established, to restrict contact between Muslim and non-Muslim areas

1926 Gezira cotton-growing scheme begins

1940s Pressure for independence

1955 Mutiny of the Equatorial Corps

1956 Independence

1958 General Abboud takes over from disorganised democratic government

1961 Civil war begins in the south

1964 Abboud gives up power after failing to solve economic problems and end war in the south

1965 Coalition civilian government formed

1969 Colonel Nimeiri takes power, promising socialist path

1970s Ambitious development programmes start

1971 Communist-inspired coup attempt; Nimeiri begins rightward shift

1972 Addis Ababa Accord signed to end civil war, promising development and autonomy for the south

1973 Arab oil prices rise

1980s Debts spiral, output falls, prices rise

1983 Southern soldiers mutiny; new rebellion begins; Nimeiri introduces *shar'ia* (Islamic law)

1985- Military takeover after Nimeiri
1986 deposed in popular uprising. Election leads to coalition government.

1989 30 June: Army coup, led by Brigadier el-Bashir, backed by the National Islamic Front

Sudan: facts and figures

Land area 2,376,000 sq. km

Population 27.3 million (1993 estimate), estimated to be growing at 2.8% each year

Ethnic groups 19 major groups, 597 sub-groups

Religions c. 60% Muslim; c. 15% Christian; c. 25% traditional faiths

Languages Arabic (spoken by 60% of population) is the official language; English is the lingua franca in the south. 115 tribal languages are spoken.

Literacy 45% for men, 13% for women (1992 estimates)

Life expectancy 53 years (1993 estimate); infant mortality is 77 per 1,000

Currency Sudanese pounds. S£760 = US$1 (official rate, 1995)

External debt $16.5 billion (1993)

Gross Domestic Product $456.20m (1993)

Inflation rate 143 per cent (1994)

Top three exports Cotton ($179m), sesame ($54m), gum arabic ($45m)

Top three imports Petroleum products ($315m), manufactured goods ($69m), machinery and equipment ($63m)

(Source: *Country Profile*, Economist Intelligence Unit, 1996)

Boys playing in Akot

CRISPIN HUGHES/OXFAM

Oxfam in Sudan

Oxfam UK and Ireland was first active in Sudan in the early 1980s, with support for Ugandan refugees in southern Sudan. This programme was managed from Nairobi, but in 1984 a field office was established in Khartoum. The programme expanded rapidly during the 1984/85 famine, when Oxfam contributed to the international relief operations in Darfur, Kordofan, and Red Sea State.

In 1989, with the escalation of the civil conflict in south, Oxfam decided to extend its support into the non-government controlled areas of the south. This southern-sector programme operates under the umbrella of Operation Lifeline Sudan from Nairobi. A base at Lokichokio, in northern Kenya, provides logistical support, including air-lift capacity and a depot for supplies.

The overall aim of Oxfam UK and Ireland in its work in Sudan is to support and build the capacity of marginalised and vulnerable communities affected by the current conflict.

In Northern Darfur and Red Sea State, our relief operations are evolving towards long-term community-development programmes, working alongside village-development committees, in the sectors of water supply, health, education, and food security. In Juba, Bahr el Jabal State, Oxfam works on relief projects through a consortium of agencies, and is helping returning rural populations to re-establish themselves. In the Khartoum urban programme, partner agencies, working with displaced communities, are funded in the fields of income-generation, revolving credit schemes, and family reunification.

In non-government controlled areas, Oxfam works to rehabilitate the most vulnerable populations through an integrated programme combining water-supply, health-care, and food-security measures. In Western Equatoria, Oxfam concentrates on agricultural and social development, working alongside co-operatives and local women's groups. Throughout Sudan, with the support of Oxfam, paraveterinary programmes operate revolving drug funds for the benefit of pastoralist and agro-pastoralist communities.

In 1994/95, Oxfam made grants worth more than £2,650,000 to relief and development work in Sudan.

An Oxfam-funded well in Akot, Rumbek County
CRISPIN HUGHES/OXFAM

Opposite page: An Oxfam-funded co-operative in Rumbek County

Further reading

Africa Watch, *Civilian Devastation. Abuses by All Parties in the War in Southern Sudan*, New York, Washington, Los Angeles, London, 1994

African Rights, *Sudan's Invisible Citizens. The Policy of Abuse Against Displaced People in the North*, London, 1995

African Rights, *Facing Genocide: the Nuba of Sudan*, London, 1995

Al-Affendi, Abd el-Wahab, *Tourabi's Revolution: Islam and Power in Sudan*, London, 1991

Allen, T. (ed.), *In Search of Cool Ground: Displacement and Homecoming in Northeast Africa*, London: James Currey, 1996

Bleuchot, C., D. Delmet, D. Hopwood (eds.), *Sudan: History, Identity, Ideology*, Reading: Ithaca Press, 1991

Burr, J.M. and R.O. Collins, *Requiem for the Sudan: War, Drought, and Disaster Relief on the Nile*, Boulder and London: Westview Press, 1995

Duffield, M., *Sudan at the Crossroads: From Emergency Preparedness to Social Security*, Institute of Development Studies, University of Sussex, 1990

Johnson, D.H. *The Root Causes of Sudan's Civil Wars*, London: James Currey, 1994

Kenyon, S., *Five Women of Sennar. Culture and Change in Central Sudan*, Oxford: Clarendon Press, 1991

Pakenham, T., *The Scramble for Africa*, London: Weidenfeld and Nicolson, 1991

Verney, P. (ed.), *Sudan: Conflict and Minorities*, London: Minority Rights Group International, 1995

Woodward, P. (ed.), *Sudan After Nimeiri*, London and New York: Routledge, 1991

MIKE WELLS/OXFAM

SPLM/A Update (bi-weekly), Nairobi
Sudan Democratic Gazette (monthly), London
Sudan Update (bi-weekly), London
Sudanow (monthly), Khartoum

(Inclusion of a book or periodical in this list of suggested reading does not necessarily imply endorsement of its contents.)

Acknowledgements

Many people in Sudan and the United Kingdom, too numerous to mention individually, contributed to the writing and production of this book. Particular thanks are due, however, to Dr Douglas Johnson for his invaluable advice on the first draft of the text, and to Crispin Hughes, for his generous provision of photographs.